Above the Veil

A Collection by Henry White II

UGLY
Publishing

Dedication

This book is dedicated to the loving memory of Henry E. White, my father. He taught me many things about life. One thing he always told me is "Life is not a dress rehearsal." So, Pop, here it is—the book many have encouraged me to write. I am now offering to the world. I love you.

Prologue

I traversed the waters of emotions and their many origins. I enjoyed the beauty and essence of love. I experienced disappointment, loss and pain. Along the way, I kept a poetic journal of love, coping, despair, redemption and hope. Now I share this authentic, poignant view of my human condition with you.

Part I

Eros

Abyss

The allure of this inscrutable force is almost magnetic
If I say it won't end well, I would seem prophetic
    I've felt the deleterious sensation in the past, and thus
    One would assume by this time I'd be smart enough
Not to get entangled in this quandary beyond aesthetics
    Why did I believe I would be loved?

Yet without hesitation, recalcitrance or resistance
I aimlessly follow the scent of love, and it's senseless
    This time feeling it is real, or so it seems in my soul
    Hoping endless euphoria is how this will unfold
Being a fool for love is my instinctive penchant
    Oh, how many times do I have to languish in this
    role?

Foolishly hoping she'll do what she committed
That when she told me she loved me, she actually meant it
    Instead, it's concealed with kisses, bogus claims
    And concludes in seemingly Sisyphean pain
If she has no desire, why can't she admit it?
    Maybe she relishes playing this game

I want to tell her I love her, but I'm scared. What will
happen?
Why does she want my heart to be a bottomless chasm?
    Each has taken a piece of my heart when she left
    But never left a piece of hers for me to possess
Their words are never validated by actions
Now all I have is an empty cavity inside my chest

Does she hate me so much that she enjoys my demise?
Or just trying to see if I'll believe all her lies?
Of course, I don't, but my love for her is so intense
And I want to believe she has sincere intent
But instead, I ponder alone, tears well in my eyes
A fool for love again fell into the abyss

Perez

Your face is lovely and comely
Seeing you is pure pleasure
You are like uncut diamonds
But she doesn't know she has a treasure
Buried inside, not something you can measure
You need nothing to make you look more beautiful or better
You are alluring as you are
One of the most beautiful, by far

Willow

I don't know why and I really can't explain
Why for the last couple of months or so,
You've been pervasive in my brain
I already know it's insane
Embarking on a losing game
I know your intentions are never to hurt
You are too sweet to profane
Maybe that's why my feelings have grown
Like the trunk of a willow, but they weep, you know
But that's not for you to be concerned about
It's my responsibility; I have to work it out
I know we're just friends and we're cool and all
And that we shouldn't really get too involved
But I still think about you, I love you so much
I wish I was the one feeling your loving touch
In the end, I know it's just a fantasy
You already have a man and really we
Should continue to be friends
But my heart skips a beat even when
I get a text or phone call and it's from you
I can't believe it's true
But I'm falling in love with you

Beautiful

I know your heart has been broken
And part of you feels like it's been stolen
But you are beautiful
So beautiful, it's unusual
You can be rich or poor, sick or healthy and well
In any instance, I'm captivated by your spell
You are simply beautiful
For me, being smitten isn't usual
One day soon your fragile heart will heal
You'll look back on the pain you now feel
And realize you are beautiful
You are definitely not the usual
A precious stone encased in gold
Your pulchritude just never seems to grow old
Your beauty is captivating
My breath is escaping

Becky

I miss your brown skin
I miss my Mexican
I miss your long hair
And your long chin
I miss all of your smart-ass anecdotes
How you would say YAY YUH!…and I quote (unquote)
And your look when you tilt your head and wink your eye
And how you went crazy when I squeezed your thigh
I miss your turtles and your butterflies
Seeing you, my stomach always gets butterflies
I miss your tulips and your Chinese roses
And how you twitched and giggled when I pinched your nose
I miss your morning breath
I miss your clumsy steps
I miss your awkward walk
And your pneumatic chest
I miss my sweet, brown sugar gingerbread
I miss waking up next to you in the bed
Just to start the morning with you in my arms
I miss you sleeping straight through your phone's alarm
I miss all the nights you would call my phone
Just to tell me, you were chilling at home alone
And I could come through just to chill with you
So we cuddled on the couch and caught a movie or two
I miss your Moroccan soap and your pink sponge
And you wearing Doc Martens trying to look grunge
I miss you telling me I'm a rare find
I miss you saying if I would have you, you would be mine
I miss you coming over late in your pjs
Trying to make the point clear that you plan to stay
I miss kissing you as the snow falls

I miss you drinking Mick Ultra out of long straws
I miss you fartin' then acting like you didn't do it
I like seeing you set a goal and stubbornly pursue it
Not gonna mention all the nights we got intimate
'Cause I know you and my sheets still remember it (will never forget)
Was doing laundry two, three times a week
Those are the only words about it that I will speak
I miss your loud snores and your downpours ;)
And how you'd say you would stay two hours more
Then you came to bed wearing your socks (Umm)
My Sinn watch would get caught in your locks (I know not really for you)
I know you hated it, you would bitch, too
But always end the night saying, "I love you"
Before you went to sleep
No anger kept (So I thought)
As I admired your beauty while you slept
And in the morning, it was the same…truly
That's why I always complimented you on your natural beauty
I miss the chance to chill with you in the Colony
Ask me about SOME DAY I used to say, probably
I miss your text messages with the smiley faces
I miss the chance to go with you to overseas places
Trafalgar Square, Big Ben, Windsor by the day
Then Eiffel Tower, long kisses at the Champs Élysées
Could've been a ring…maybe, after we…
        …now I can only give you one on your Galaxy…
So many days that, I reminisce of you
Sometimes, I wonder if you really think about me, too
'Cause that was a while back, but I still miss you
And you'd be lying if you said you didn't miss me, too
Your soft lips, I like to kiss them, too
You'd be lying if you said you didn't miss mine, too

Daydream

The birds wake early to sing her praises
       She who walks through my dreams every night
And fills my thoughts throughout the day
       Whose glory is like the sun at its height
Such beauty I beckon, but hide from her rays
       Her countenance is such a glorious sight
Inviting her even to come out and play
       In hopes that my inner self she will like
But not knowing exactly the right words to say
       And shrieking with wonder, fear and delight
I calmly reserve myself in her presence
       How do I maintain in her absence?
Her lips intoxicating me like absinthe
Will I ever kiss her heart and caress her essence?

Delilah

Whose eyes that shine
Whose caress is but an apparition
For whom I write this rhyme
Her body language weighted with indecision
But her gentle countenance seizes time
Whose soul is ripe
For the deluge of senses
As embers of Lebanon
She blossoms as roses
In a moist garden
Her smile, her chortle, her coyish laugh
To my ears pleasantly mellifluous
Her tender breast, to my breath, a gasp
For my eyes, this sight is propitious
Her silhouette exuded class
I long to kiss her heart at its core
And touch her emotions like none before

Despair

I wish on no man the depths of despair
The flight of the weary
The plight of the lonely
And so many do not care
The life of the depressed
The world of the despised
The pain of broken hearts
Love's demise
The loss of a loved one
The feeling of betrayal
Being taken for granted
A love that failed
The nights of solitude
The days of anguish
The fear of repeating
Being the loving fool
The care that is given
But not reciprocated
Efforts unappreciated
While one goes on living
The other hurts alone
The walls are closing in
Life seems different now
Feeling like an alien at home
Everything to remind him
Of what could have been
The times that meant so much
Are hard to put behind him
But for the other it didn't mean very much
The times he sorely misses

Were but a diversion
But he misses her tender touch
That in hindsight wasn't tender
It was not at all sincere
The times he wants to cherish
She wants not to remember
One who gives all their heart
To one who enjoys breaking it to pieces
And laugh because it has no value
While he's being torn apart
I don't wish this pain on any living being
Being disposed of as nothing
Giving and not receiving
I have come to see, this is what love truly means

Farce

Your lips say they love me
But your heart is far from me
Your mind is somewhere else
Tell me where I failed
When I behold your beauty
I want to draw you close to me
But I sit here all alone all by myself

In the end, truth be told
Your heart has turned cold
You're just scared to walk away
To shake the comfort of your soul
Knowing that you have me here
Though you wish you were there
Wanting to leave but afraid to let go

You're texting me with X's and O's
Smiley faces and sweet nothings
But in my heart, I already know
You checked out a long time ago
Grinning at me while you're guffing
Your eyes try to hide the lie
In your heart, I don't reside…

…Anymore
But you won't speak the words
And woe is me if I tell you I notice
Hissing, you say it's absurd
Daydreaming, I believe is the verb
Lying with me, but he is your focus
Now hope for me is truly hopeless
Knowing one day soon you'll return

To him that is, eh'hem, of course
I dare not think I have your love
With you two, it's an impenetrable force
One I'd be a fool to fight
I gave my all, but not enough
I love you, but I must close the doors
I kiss you, then disappear in the night

Feelings

The sun's going down
And I'm sitting around
Wondering why I feel the way I do
Why do I love you?

It doesn't seem to make much sense
The grass is always greener inside the fence
I'm so confused
Why do I love you?

I never saw this coming
The day it dawned on me
I thought you were the one
Yes, it is true
I'm in love with you

I can't tell you though
Because we're just friends
And that's a love affair
I don't want to end
Don't want to lose you
Because I truly love you

But my heart keeps burning
Deep inside my chest
When I see you smile
Yes, I must confess
I really want to
Tell you I love you

I want to hold you in my arms so tight
And keep you warm
All through the rainy nights
I am such a fool
To fall in love with you

For Me

How many times have I cried myself to sleep?
For a girl to love me, even if only for a week
Who will shun all other fellows just for me?
Even if it happens to be Brad Pitt or George Clooney

I know that's not a real possibility
Who can stay around after seeing the real me?
Why did this calamity have to be for me?
Why am I strange, eccentric and ugly?

It must have been something I did long ago
That makes me go to bed every night all alone
If I was never born, this pain I'd have never known
So, I drink until all the feelings are gone

Muse...(For Whom I Write)

Behold, her amber countenance divine
  Her neck like ivory tower to taste
Of the lips like goblets of aged wine
  And threads of silk locks that frame her face
  Glory's her essence, perfection and grace

Fairest is she among all in her presence
  Her breath the fragrance of apples and such
Whose eyes are like gems, both rare and precious
  Many do long to drink from her cup
  And it's amazing her hand just to touch

Peach

They say the best is yet to come
    I'm not sure I can concur
Could I find the best when I'm so young?
    But undoubtedly, I found her
Seething at what I'd then become
How can I find another if she's the one?

It seems I picked a peach
    When climbing the tree of life
Whose nectar is so sweet
    And fruit from the bough so ripe
Yet never to taste inside my cheek
Her exquisite nectar always seemed out of reach

Of me that is, I love my dear
    Which I'd picked from the climb
Whose nectar formed a solemn tear
    For being picked before its time
But none can correct past errs
I just wish my peach were here, not there

She's probably blossomed, a beautiful garden
    As some man's delightful wife
This could have grown, if I was smarter
    And been the sweet nectar of my life
The most perfect thing I ever started
Rewarded me by leaving me brokenhearted

Pink Plains of Solitude

I've kissed the impulsive thoughts of a goddess
Made love to the majestic mind of a queen
I've licked the lascivious emotions of a princess
Only to realize it was merely a dream
Nothing in life is quite what it seems

I've played freely on the pink plains of affection
Perched snuggly with robins and flown with passerines
Sailed a vessel on the river's rapidly rushing streams
Only to realize it was merely a dream
Nothing in life is quite what it seems

She's Not Here

I can still smell her perfume
Her roses remain on the table
I wait for her to walk into the room
But she's not here, it's all in my mind

I keep waiting by the phone
Hoping she will call
I cry every time I hear our song
But she's not here, it's all in my mind

I wake up and say, "Hey baby"
But the pillow never replies
My friends think I'm going crazy
'Cause she's not here and I'm losing my mind

Where did I go wrong?
What in the world did I do?
How could I be so good to her
And still lose?
Why are the nights so lonely?
And my days spent confused?
What did I do to deserve this pain?
She's not here, so where is she?

Is another man lying in her bed
While I wake up alone?
I can't get this out of my head
Because she's not here, it's all in my mind

Will my baby ever come back to me?
How long should I wait for her return?
How long will this pain belong to me?
She's not here, and she may never come back

I did everything a man could for her love
Was there for her when times got rough
But maybe it just wasn't enough
Cause she's not here

Southern Belle

On amber waves of grain
Across the Texas plains
There was a lovely Southern belle
That I thought I knew so well
But she filled my days with pain

And another seemed the same
One's loss was another's gain
She was a lovely Southern belle
I wanted to know so well
She replaced cloudy days with rain

Flowers blossom in the springtime
One I love, the other is in the meantime
But autumn came so soon
And dawn was quickly noon
And the sun faded into nighttime

She shined like the brightest star
Lighting my night even from afar
Far, far south from where I am
But she never seemed to give a damn
She never took care of my heart

She had a glimpse of a chance
To have my heart in her hand
This lovely Southern belle
Wishes she hadn't failed
A poor victim of circumstance

If only she'd a clue
Of what my love could do
But this lovely Southern belle
Showed her nasty true self
So the flower never blossomed or grew

She did something similar
Hurt my heart in particular
Too busy to stop and ask
How our roads could cross paths
Theirs was perpendicular

With me at the center, I should've known
All I wanted was "I love u and I'll be home"
But I asked for a bit too much
I was a bit too out of touch
So she left me to be all alone

Like the dusk's sun, a beautiful crimson
Reflects from her gentle countenance and glistens
She is a lovely Southern belle
Whose love I tried to have but failed
But that won't stop me from wishing

The Songbird

Red is her color from name and origin
    Lovely is this wondrous bird in flight
Bubbly as Clicquot, she's steadily pouring
    A glimpse of sensuous *vino* in sight
Anointing this rhyme…this complex conundrum
    A beautiful puzzle no one can reveal
Of those who attempt will only succumb
    D'ailleurs don't even try, you're sure to fail
Alas, her very essence is embedded in these lines
    Comeliness on the other hand, could never be covert
Pulchritude, in itself, describes the perky passerine
    I cannot open to her my heart, lest it will surely be hurt
Inspiration, she is my muse, *l'objet de mon amour*
    Whose color is rouge as the dwindling sun at dawn
Son sourire apporte un sourire à mon couer
    This thrush remains the love of Wisconsin
Her disposition is by far the captor of my soul
    Appearing to be unctuous, but only in my dreams
I wrote this as a mystery, bewildered in a code
    Only the one I adore can grasp what it truly means

Elle est l'oiseau chanteur le plus bel

Untitled

Nothing could be as precious
As the sight of you
Nothing could be as fulfilling
As your beautiful smile
In my parlance, I described
Those lips as ripe pomegranate
The coquette for whom my heart
Springs passion
Torrents of lust & Eros
Unbelievable in every graceful step
While I admire
As I conceal my desire
The fire that burns within
Is love's unquenchable thirst

Valentine

Delightful is she is all her glory
    Wishing she was still mine to clutch
Meant for me, it's not the end of the story
    I cannot forget all the magical times we touched
She's an angel from heaven, a sight to behold
    Can she figure out the puzzle hidden in these lines?
Can I tell her how I love her body and soul?
    Henry, smiles when she smiles all the time
You are my Zipporah, I'm your Moses, my love
    You are by far the captor of my heart
I love Elizabeth, my whimsical, tender dove
    There's not one thing in this world to tear us apart
You, be my Valentine, my brown-sugar gingerbread…
    Diana has all my heart and my head

Vapor

I really knew it from the very start
I was embarking on a crazy game
I knew I'd end up with a broken heart
But yet and still, I decided to play

At one point, I looked good in the score
In control and feeling much in charge
But I was in for oohhh so much more
And I still fell short in my repechage

Just when I thought that it was in my grasp
It disappeared just like a vapor…gas
And when I thought that it is was mine for sure
I realized that it was just a vapor

I did my best to try and seize the day
I'm not sure what more I could've done
Was my love remiss in any way?
I guess I always knew this day would come

Now I feel hurt, confused, lonely and dumb
This pain's intense, but yet and still, it's strange
That, though I knew one day that I'd be shunned
I left my heart open to feel this pain

I wonder how long will this heartbreak last
I always knew that it was vapor…gas
Who would've known the pain that I'd endure
She just disappeared just like a vapor

Will she come back, or just go back?
These crazy thoughts are driving me insane
It's just so hard for me to face the fact
I'm not the one that's always on her brain

My ship is sinking and I'm fading fast
Into thin air, just like a vapor…gas
I don't think that I can take much more
She just disappeared like a vapor

Baiser

Was it our first and last kiss?
Or was it my last first kiss?
My sweet cherry blossom
Whose lips I long to touch with mine
Consuming my thoughts
With her clutching me against her bosom
And passion that only grows over time
Will she recklessly give me her heart?

Was it my last first kiss?
Or kiss that went amiss?
Will she throw caution to the wind?
As it seems I have myself
Willing to risk heartbreak
Or will it be happy in the end?
Like a royal flush that was dealt
Or am I making a grave mistake?

Was it my last first kiss?
Or the last time to drink of her lips?
My mind is replete with questions
Solemnly fraught with suspicions
Doubt, trepidation and fear reign
In all of this, was there a lesson?
Will she be able to share my vision?
Or was it all done in vain?

Was it my last first kiss?
Could she love someone like this?
Me, a miscreant, eccentric

Am I pervasive in her mind?
Was it random or was it fate?
What are her true intentions?
To drop her guard and be mine?
Is this really love beginning to take shape?

Weekend

What was I thinking when I brought you to Dallas?
When she asked if she could stay at my palace?
Thought the trip would be somewhat enlightening
But the days leading up were quite frightening
Saw her face, intense emotions are heightening
I'm nervous and don't know why, for the life of me
She likes me or she wouldn't be here in the first place
She flew 1200 miles to go on our first date
Everything was first rate, I'm thinking the worst case
That she gets bored, wants to leave, maybe a little this irks
me
Though, I can say I never anticipated
That by Saturday she'd be thoroughly irritated
I'm trying to break through and getting frustrated
Almost threw my hands up and capitulated
But dinner came Saturday, it was Valentine's Day
Roses, Cabernet and Ferrero Rocher
She said it's her favorite, so that's how I played it
Laid dinner out gentlemanly, dinner finally saved it
Now, I'll see if she really wants more of me
Or when I call and text, will she be ignoring me?
I wanna see just what's in store for me
But is she home now and through with exploring me?

Who Is It?

She comes in at *dusk*
But leaves before dawn
She sometimes arrives
Disguised as *lust*
At times when life leaves
One in *disgust,*
She rigidly cleaves
to the strings of one's heart
But she will quickly depart
and act as if she's never seen?
We've all had her before
Some more than the rest
Yet she is no whore
And those who claim
To have had her before
May even call her by name
Simply have her confused
With someone much less
For once she truly has you
There is no *next*
She is the only
In many forms
Maybe it's her shape
That is never deformed
Some contort her true essence
Though at heart she is *pure*
Her intensity chases away sleep
She can be right beside you
Yet you feel so alone
To the point you can't even eat

She is the *cure* to all ills
Still, she makes you sick
Until you wish to die
For her, some kill
For her, some steal
Others lay down their own life
There is no high
To rival the thrill
Of how she makes you feel so alive
She turns geniuses to idiots
Socialites to introverts
Giants into midgets
All are addicted to how she feels
When this princess kisses your neck
When it's cold, she warms your soul
Her sensuous touch is more than sex
It's more than Eros, more than passion
Nothing can ever compare
To her in action
Inevitably men and women fall captive
To her, this beauty who has no race
She is *soooooo* beautiful
And always with you
But some can't seem to trace
She spreads herself about the world
Never in one place
At a time
She is too universal
She always remains poised
Yet seems so unrehearsed
She's been the purpose
Of myriad rhymes
Irrational decisions
Wars among men

Scuffles among women
I cannot seem to grasp her fully
Though she is my life's work
Who I hopelessly chase
But never behold her beautiful face
Who is she?

Part II

Black Dog

Able

Have you ever felt unlovable?
Walking the streets like a loathsome epiphany
In anonymity that is really ubiquity
Everyone can see through to your iniquity
Then suddenly I see a smile, but realize
They're laughing at me and not with me
Have you ever felt forgettable?
Like the day the earth conceived you was regrettable?
Why you even exist is ineffable
Feeling your goodness is untestable
Because it doesn't exist, then you realize
Why you are utterly detestable?
Have you ever felt despicable?
Where the urge to hate you is irresistible
When your pregnant ego is permissible
Even when it won't give birth is admissible
Resisting the inevitability of life's vicissitudes

Eyes

I saw this young girl the other night
She looked at me, said she saw pain in my eyes
I played it off, dropped some Visine in and told her I'd been crying
She told me there's no need for lying
She could see something deeper inside
And my eyes won't allow me to hide

Fly Away

I spread my wings to fly and be free
But I always make sure my loved ones are with me
None of my flock are still in the tree
Everywhere I go you are with me
But if I die today
Those other birds will just fly away
When I cry today
Those other birds just fly away
At my old age, my wings are tattered
And my beak is feeling weak
My feathers are scattered
And my claws are shattered
For never having shoes on my feet
But if I die today
Would the other birds just fly away?
If I die today
Would any of them cry today?
So now I go this alone
My babies are all grown
And now I have to take all my flights on my own
But if I die today
They will just fly away
Would they even remember me?
Or will I be a distant memory?
When I cry today
Will they all hide away?

Friday 13, 2020

Every moment I muddle through the days, I can hear
The backstrokes of pain as I swim in puddles of tears
And every week seems interminable, like hundreds of years
And the Irish nectar was a friend because it numbed my fears
It dumbed down my thoughts, gave light to my emotions
It's dark inside this cavern, I'm just dying in slow motion
I'm crying and hopeful in God's loving devotion
A quiet still of peace when my life is in commotion
And my cries can fill an ocean
My pride is a haughty notion
When I'm trying to remain focused
I pray to my Holy Father
And get drenched in Holy water
Sometimes I muse and ponder
And then I wonder, why bother?
If this shadow following me is leading me to slaughter
I bow my head to my Abba
And hope He answers graciously
I keep hope for a better tomorrow
And ask that you pray for me

Heart's Fears

My imperfections have been laid bare
For the audience to see and hear
But my heart still fights strife and fear
Of leaving this world with no one aware
On dark streets and desolate bars filled with lovely, lonely souls
In empty homes, on television sets displaying the final score
In crowded offices where I often go
But I desire that style of life no more
I long to be with my partner on beautiful shores
I feel like my blessing has come in arrears
As if I did my life's due diligence and it's finally near
I believe it is, but is my vision unclear?
No, I have it; it is simply the turmoil that my heart fears

Hidden Room

There is a place where many arrive
Some leave for better things
Some stay the rest of their lives
None like what the room brings
It is dark and there is no light
No paintings or decorations
No illumination in sight
Only lamentations
When you're there, you don't realize
That there are other guests as well
It's like seeking with closed eyes
No water is in the well
Yet tears flood this room
Pain is its sole purpose
It contains terror, fear and doom
The people feel hopeless, lost and worthless
Yet you cannot see them
And neither can you be seen
It leaves an empty feeling within
But all is not what it seems
Loved ones find you there
They seek to love, but you are clandestine
It seems appears that no one cares
And this room is where you are destined
When leaving this macabre place
There are only two destinations
One is final, the end of the race
The other an undisclosed location
I've been there many times before
I have been blessed to escape
Yet I seem to go back for more

When things are not going great
As I reach for the door
I can't help but wonder, why?
What did I come back for?
Is it to see hopelessness, pain and cries?
Tears from those with so much
To offer, so many hearts to heal
Who don't feel love's touch
Or maybe just too numb to feel
Lacerated hearts, disappointed souls
Broken spirits, unmet expectations
Losers at love, unachieved goals
Destroyed by degradation
This room is not a happy place
And no one wants to go, in fact
This room is never without space
Yet it is always packed
But now it really seems as if
I am on my return journey
The door is open, I take a sniff
Ahh the familiar smell of pain and hurting'

Hollow

I've been hurt so much that my soul feels hollow
So I fill it with alcohol and love that turns to sorrow
Crying myself to sleep simply thinking about tomorrow
And all the phony smiles and fake affection I have to borrow
Just to make it through the day, I mean fake it through the
day
All my life, dreams have been taken away
Without payment to me, my heart was grifted
With no way for my soul to be uplifted
Because it's hollow

Holli Coca

I met her at a party when I was seventeen
Wasn't an instant spark, she treated me kind of mean
The next day, I wondered what I had done
Didn't see her again for over a year
Not knowing she would soon be my dear
At graduation she was looking real grand
So excited, I reached out to take her hand
She took mine and we went out to the floor
We danced and kissed and had a wonderful time
But I still wasn't trying to make her mine
Then off to college. She was everywhere
Oh, how she'd grown, I just stopped and stared
At her beauty and grandiloquence, lo and behold
We grew closer, but at the time this girl Mary was my muse
She kept telling me it was her I should choose
Over the years, we stayed close, but Mary was still my dear
We kept in touch, and all along she kept whispering in my
ear
How no one could love me the way she does
I must admit, that wasn't when I first began pondering
But Mary started acting bad and got me to wondering
I had to tell Mary with tears running down my cheek
That she had changed so much it's best we didn't speak
So I called up Mary, still not sure why
And began a romance we still have to this day
I try not to, but I see her almost every day
I drink in her aroma and I'm sucked in
She stays with me every night until I'm sleepy and tucked in
But now I'm having second thoughts about what I'm doing
She reassures me she will always be around
And true, she was always there when the chips were down
But then making love started to feel like strain

Where I would wake in the morning with this intense pain
She said she'd cure me when I came to see her one night
Like a fool, I ran to her, but it seemed like work
When he greeted me at the door with her sly, cagey smirk
Whenever I called, she came, no matter time or location
On every occasion, depression or celebration
Until I started feeling like she was crowding me a little
But she reassured me that she loved me so
And how she'd always bring me comfort if I didn't let her go
But now I'm at a crossroads because she keeps me broke
Thinking about calling Mary to catch up on times of old
But she is probably married with a happy life
Here I am stuck with that gold digger playing with my head
But oh, how she sparkles in that dress when she wears red
Enough is enough; I have to tell her we're finished
Another girl or not, I'm out; I'm done with this jail sentence
I hope she doesn't track me down to kill me later in life
I've got to move on now while at least I still have health
I wouldn't wish this evil stalking woman on anyone else

I Was Told

I was once told that love is blind
And this is something that I have come find
True in its simplicity
But only through pain can one know
And heal the wounds with time
I was told that lovers are kind
And that true love is hard to find
But it is even harder to keep
But when it really works
The sun could not outshine it
I was told to love like I've never been hurt
That lust is a feeling and love is work
I've found this is true as well
Few wiser words have ever been spoken
But sometimes I wonder, is the pain really worth it?
I was told that pain reminds you you're alive
Because you feel no more pain once you die
But sometimes pain is so intense
You don't know if you can handle it
Though you always have to try
I was told to look inside myself
That the heart is truly the measure of wealth
That all the riches the world over
Cannot replace a heart of gold
Which I have, but gold can melt
I once knew a wise man full of proverbs
And he uttered these sagacious words
Someone who loves you won't make you cry
And someone who does is not worth the tears
Those are some of the wisest words I've ever heard
But I've cried many tears

I've been let down over the years
Yet I still give out my heart
As if it were a pamphlet
My weakness is being sincere
I was told to love many and trust few
Always paddle your own canoe
My grandma told me this a long time ago
If I would've learned the lesson
I wouldn't be as I am now, a sullen lonely fool

Loneliness

When the loneliness sets in the like the lodger
That came to stay for a few weeks
But now it's months later and
I realize they're not trying to leave
When pangs of isolation feel like four walls
Closing in as I gasp for air
I wait by the phone, but no one calls
And I begin to wonder if anyone cares
Like feet firmly planted in quicksand
A slow descent as I sink into the quagmire
Of this depraved wasteland where I now find myself
It steals my love, motivation, and desire
When all I can do is drink to numb the pain
And all the emotions I feel are laid bare
Insane thoughts invade my racing brain
As I wish someone were here, not there
It doesn't seem fair; it feels quite unjust
Do they only love what I can do for them?
And not me for who I am?
Am I being a paranoid wreck again?
As I sit in a room full of people
Not feeling like part of the group
I hear their voices, clinking glasses and joyous laughs
In my mind, I'm alone in my dark room
What first originated in my youth
Is something I thought I'd grow out of
But instead, only got accustomed to
And to this day, I'm unable to rise above
Feeling out of place wherever I happen to be
Am I insecure or is it low self-esteem?
Am I an outsider? Is that how they view me?

And I doubt my own sanity, which leads me to this requiem
I wish it were only a nightmare, a bad dream
Then I could wake in the morn to a brand-new start
But unfortunately, it's my genuine existence
It's the temporary lodger that refuses to depart

Birthday

A young lady told me to offer my writing to the world
I'm sitting here thinking, should I take advice from a little girl?
But she is wise beyond her years with a lot left to ascertain
She's correct in her assessment that I have something for the world to gain
I don't look at my words as anything influential
To me, it's my sounding board that to others is inconsequential
I'm flattered, but I hate to hear that I have so much potential
When does that shit turn kinetic?
When the fuck am I gonna get out of my fog and finally get it?
Or is there anything to really get?
Just love, heartbreak and more bullshit
Just being taken for granted and not appreciated
I'm kind of over this shit
I love my son and my nephew
But they made the mistake of loving this dude
I know many say that I'm too sensitive
I'm sorry, I just happen to love, maybe, too intense
I do stupid shit that doesn't make sense
I hate to disappoint people who love me, it makes my heart hurt
I'm contemplating life and what this bullshit is really worth
I'm sick of waking up feeling depressed
Wishing that every day was the last day
Constantly fighting these demons that never go away
No one seems to believe I'm sitting, dying over here
They don't understand how much time I spend crying over here
They think I'm playing or just lying over here

My runway is short, can I have someone just to lie with me over here?

I want a sincere, intimate touch
But apparently that's asking too much
I just want you to love me
I may be a scrub but, but my spirit is lovely
And I really do love my God who is above me

Near the End

All nights seem cold and lonely
Because I'm chilling with the one and only me
Not chilling with my lovely
Because she doesn't want to be with me
And truth be told, neither does anybody else
Why am I stuck in this room with my thoughts and myself?
And my thoughts often venture to suicide
Thinking who would be at my funeral and who would cry?
Who would give a shit and who would notice after food is
served?
I spent much of my life sacrificing, that's my word
And all I got was a stabbed back and fake love
Except for my God sitting up above
The sphere of the earth, said the book of Isaiah
But my mental dysfunction comes in multiple layers
To the point, I can't blame any girl for bailing
I know I'm going to heaven but I'm living in hell
Currently, as though I seem to have enough currency
I'm living my life with this frantic sense of urgency
I'm drinking and smoking
Hoping to kill myself
By the time I enjoy life, that's when I'm going
I really hope this ain't a prophecy that's self-fulfilling
I'm just a hurting soul in serious need of healing
Feeling the steady pain of rejection and despondence
Until I can't even respond to the women that's calling
I'm balling, I'll buy a big house to be alone in it
And drive around alone in my new Benz and shit
I just want to give the most to my girlfriend
But soon or later, it's the end
I read the last chapter in the book
Just procrastinating, delaying reading to get another look

I admit, I've stolen many hearts, I was a crook
So maybe this is the payback
So maybe I should lay back
And endure it
Don't say that, be mature
For sure, I'm thinking I may lack
The mental capacity for sure
'Cause I'm damn good at getting took
But I'm sure I deserve it
Look at me, a fucking piece of shit and worthless
You can put dollar figures next to my name
But what's the purpose?
Was I on purpose or an accident?
I know I'm not the only one asking this
I see you all laughing and shit
And it's at me
I could go on the attack
But I should attack me, harass me
Cause I'm out front
But who's got my back…me?
Sometimes I'm tacky
Lacking common sense
So just wrap me in an electrical razor wire fence
That's what's happening
My death shouldn't be happy
Since my life ain't
I'm sick of talking, sick of writing
Here's my last quote
So, you can take this as my suicide note

No Subject

My life is a cosmic, tragic comedy
Where everyone points at me
Where everyone looks and laughs at me
Where God looks down, it seems
He frowns at me
Watches me mess up my life and laughs at me
That hurts me
I love God
Why does He want me to suffer?
For once, I'd like to have something that isn't broken
Something that actually works like it supposed to

Perilous Road

Just another lost soul on this perilous road
I explore alternate ways to pontificate
Its existence from my existing being
But all my feckless efforts leave me alone
If I am misled, I wish someone would indicate
Chase away the horror that my eyes and heart have seen
It seems as if all of my phonetic responses no
To searching for something my mind creatively facilitates
And find love that exists outside of my dreams

Shades

I wear my shades a lot
To hide my eyes a lot
To hide what lies beneath this façade I've got
To hide the fact that, yeah, I cry a lot
The hurt deep inside just never seems to stop
But if I show it, they'll just exploit it for their gain
Make my life a punch line and laugh at my pain
I'm depressed every day
How do I maintain?
Is God holding me by a thread? Can someone please explain?
This couldn't possibly be healthy for my brain
Or my heart for that matter
There isn't a day I don't wake up sadder
Than the day before
I feel one day I'll explode
So I just put on my shades so no one will ever know
I accomplish enough to get a temporary glow
That's extinguished, when reality hits and I am, again, alone

This Friend of Mine

This man follows me everywhere
I can't seem to make him leave
Everywhere I go, he's with me
When I go to church or on a date
Or to the bar to have a drink
He hovers over me
Never says a good word
He's always discouraging
It's like I invited him to tag along
Although I don't remember sending the invitation
He creeps up when I listen to certain songs
Makes me feel like everything I do is wrong
He won't let me be happy for long
He always reminds me of my past wrongs
He never leaves me, that's why
I may as well call him my friend
But he's destructive
He makes me think that I'm worthless
People say I have a lot going for me
How I touch people's lives
But this friend always touches mine
And his caress is never kind
I wish I could shake him
Some even tell me
Conversations on a sofa would help
But I just can't see it
Every day is a living hell
When I accomplish something
He tells me I should've done better
When I fail, he tells me it's only the beginning
He tells me I'll never amount to anything

Sometimes, I believe him
It's scary, I can't see him
But feel him in the depths of my being
He never leaves, he tells me things
I shouldn't listen to
He tells me I'm unlovable
He tells me I'm a failure
He tells me I'm a loser
He tells me I'll never rise above
Most days I try to ignore him
And go about doing the things I should
Others, he bends my ear, and I listen
He makes me insecure
He makes me feel worthless
Like I'll never have anything meaningful
It's hard fighting him every day
This friend, he never leaves
I've tried everything
Sometimes, I can't hear him for days
Sometimes, he's all I hear
He makes me think the end is near
It's scary, because very few understand
They can't see the man
Some days, he doesn't want me to wake up
Others, he makes me wish I were dead
He tries to kill me
But people say it's all in my head
I wish someone could help
But when I call out
He always disappears
So, people just think I'm crazy
I hear their whispers and his in my ears
Cursed be the day of my birth
Why didn't my mother abort me?

Why has God looked out for me?
Why am I His anointed?
Why was I not a miscarriage?
Or stillborn at birth
Now I live this daily pain
And no one feels my hurt
My pain is so intense, this friend
Will not show me mercy
Please take me from this place
But not to the fiery furnace
Let me have the day when
This friend leaves forever
He drowns me in alcohol
Women and endless shindigs
But I still feel him
I drink to drown him, but he laughs
Because I'm only fulfilling his purpose
Since I seem to have none
Myself, how should I proceed?
The only way to rid myself of this friend
Is to rid the world of me

Anxiety

I can't help suffering from anxiety
I can't help that the devil keeps trying me
I can't help that people lie to me
I can't help that everyone cries to me
But I can ignore those who cry to me
I can cut off those that lie to me
I can go to God when the enemy is trying me
But I can't help suffering from anxiety
I can be the shoulder for those that cry to me
I can forgive those that lie to me
I can go to God when the enemy is trying me

Veneer

Why am I so damn insecure?
This pain inside that I always endure
Not liking the picture I see in the mirror
Feeling as if I was conceived in error

I dress it up with nice Polos, Perry Ellis suits
Swiss watches, Varvatos Cologne and Cole Haan Shoes
If I didn't have these things, I'd never get noticed
I'm not very attractive, but I already know this

I'm not smart either, so I use big words
Trying to be cool when I know I'm a nerd
Self-conscious of course, not loving myself
Not liking who I am, so I chase after wealth

I got money, everyone, so drinks on me
If I didn't splurge, who would really like Henry?
So, I have to impress them in order to hide
The pain of this inferno that's burning inside

I buy my girls nice things, or I'm sure they would leave
Someone loving me for me, I just couldn't believe
So, I try to impress them in order to hide
The stew of self-hatred that's brewing inside

I push myself at work, for more money, more ascension
I strive to be noticed, and I like the recognition
All I ever really wanted was to be accepted
So I put on the veneer to keep my heart protected

Ugly as I am, I hide behind success
It's the veneer I learned to wear, and I have regrets
I'm afraid if people really knew me, I'd be rejected
Now my own mental health is negatively affected

I live my life behind a mask, and it's a living hell
I drink alcohol to become a different self
If I don't like me, how can I expect another to…
…Love this hideous inner me I keep a cover to?

Conceal what's below with the veneer above
What's under the mask, nobody would truly love
And I already know, so why bother to ask
I'll just avoid my true self and keep wearing the mask

Coast

I'm going far, far away
To a coast in Spain
On the Mediterranean
And they'll never see me again

Maybe I'll make new friends
Maybe I'll be the one that offends
It really doesn't matter in the end
It's all about the love I send

I don't know where to begin
So, I'll begin at the end
And it all ends where it begins
Does that make sense, my friend?

If you were to see it through
And look into the mirror, too
You'd get the real vision of you
And finally know what to do

I'm headed to the coast of Spain
On the Mediterranean
They'll never see me again

Mellow Green Meadows

The sun is glistening in it's beautiful sheen
And meadows call for me
To finally arrive where the grass is green
To go where no one is mean
The Mellow Green Meadows are calling for me
The day is beautiful and the hope is grand
As the meadows call for me
I tried many alternatives and held them in my hand
But how do I arrive there, where the grass is green?
When the meadows are calling for me
To not arrive too soon
Because there is no turning back
They may not be meadows but be a gloomy doom
That on in never able to retract
But the meadows are calling for me
Where the grass is always green
The meadows will hopefully give me peace of mind
A seed, first, has die to bring forth life
And that's what the meadows provide

PART III

Fog

Judas

When I see you, I want to smile
When I see you, I can run that extra mile
When I don't see you, I want to dial
Find out where you are
Hope that you aren't far
I'll scoop you up or get you a car
It's just you and me tonight, fuck going to a bar
We sit outside and look at the stars
And planets
And delineate, not taking for granted
What we both expect
I hope it's more than sex
I hope it's more than late night calls and simple texts

Judas II

I miss your face
Still, I smell you on my sheets
Your aggressive grace
How you wiggle when I tickle your feet
How you take sixteen minutes to brush your teeth
How our love making, to you, is never complete
How you never make me feel I have to compete

Judas IV

How can someone sleeping next to me always be in my
dreams?
Whenever she's at work it seems
As if it's weeks
But when she's with me it feels like minutes
This woman I love, I can't begin
To explain how her scent on my pillow drives my brain
With an irresistible urge to be with her again
I wish she were here right now so I could kiss her all over
And caress her sensual skin as we lie under covers
She entices my heart to love her
And desire her presence like none other

Lovers in Passing

I walk past this person every single day
I never get love anyway
She puts her issues on me
But she'll never work to establish "we"
It's me by myself, as always
It's me, as I am most days
She doesn't care if I live or die
Though if I died, where would she catch a ride?
I see her in passing like we're in a movie, actors
I'm never a priority, just a benefactor
I do everything for her, but I don't even matter
Just a place to sleep or when she wants a platter
When will she enter my life, never?
When will she stop thinking her diversions are clever?
I sit alone as I always do
I sit alone like she wants me to

More Lies

They're all lies
Every time you tell me you love me, it's a lie
Every time you say you want me, it's a lie

Guess what? I'm a human being with feelings
I know you're a person in need of healing
So am I, but I just get showered with lies

You don't love me, only what I do for you
You don't want my time, only what I do to you
Maybe this is what you're used to
It's cool because it has to be
You want this romance to be a tragedy
You're ashamed of me
I've grown tired of the fake shit, weary of the lies
I'm never fully loved no matter how much I try
But it is what is
It is what it is

My Girlfriend

My girl used to love me, or so I thought
But she never thought anything of me other than what I
bought
Making sure she wakes up on time
To talk to someone and give them her time
I have a two-hour limit and then she leaves
I have problems getting her to watch what I want to see
I have a problem getting her to love me for me
Why am I with her? For my own insecurities
Because I know she couldn't care less about me
If a speeding car was rolling down the street
She would push me in front of it and say, "I'm sorry"
Then go to the bar and have a drink
With all the other guys
Wouldn't come to the funeral to say goodbye
She would laugh and tell jokes to her friends
About how she's so slick, she played another dude again
When she found out I survived she wouldn't grin
She'd think of how she failed and try to do it again
She doesn't love me, she loves what I do to her
She loves what I do for her
But her love for me is never inferred
Because it doesn't exist

Hypnosis

I gave three years of my life
To her, it was a game
Afraid of her shame
Everyone else was to blame
I got caught in the lies
And burned by the flames
Of a ravenous dame
So many tears I cried
And it damaged my pride
When I finally realized
I was the one that was there by my side
It just doesn't seem to make sense
In a relationship with myself with an added expense
She never loved me, so why bother to utter the words
She never cultivated feelings except for hers
Feelings just for her
Nothing is left for her
Except chasing what she lost, that was best for her
Now the best things for me are still yet to occur
But it can only be clearer after the blur
She chased a dream in her mind that never was real
All she could get from me was my only sex appeal
Now she desperately seeks me, but I never appear
And the echoes of my silence are all she can hear
When the fog of this clears
The Son will appear
My love was burned into smoke
It left ashes of fears
But a new love approaches
It's closer than near
When I awoke from her hypnosis
And looked in the mirror

Your Fault

Hello, goodbye
I never cheat, I never lie
I love you, I hate you
You're the gleam in my eyes
You made me break my word
It's your fault I cried
You're an imbecile, you're a savant
I'm not coming back, you're all I want
I'm glad you're sober
You're the one that makes me drink
I believe you're a genius
Man, I hate when you overthink
Your creativity is your glory
We were just gonna meet for lunch
You're creating all these stories
It's your fault that I punched
Yes, you were lying on your back
But I still felt attacked
So I had to defend myself
There's nothing wrong with that
Some woman sent you a photo
We were only broke up for seven days
I only said I'd go hiking with him
That's not really a date
I'm so sick of you always playing these games
So what, I took the money, I also put in some change
I know I promised to pay rent when it came due
But I gave money to my family
And nothing was left for you
You're not my leftovers

You're my last and my first
It was the way you said it
That made me scream and curse
I love you baby, you're the best
Thanks for filling my purse
You always call me out like I'm lying
I swear, you're the worst
I'm so done with you
Why won't you answer your phone?
There must be someone there with you
And I swear I'm alone
Answer the phone
Please answer the phone!
I can't deal with reality now that you're gone
Answer the phone
Damn it! Answer the phone
So I can tell you all about how my feelings have grown
Answer the phone
ANSWER THE FUCKING PHONE
I won't accept that you left and you're moving along

Glimpse (Symphony)

Even in the darkness of night
When I could see but had no sight
It was like
The sun shining by just a glimpse of your eyes
That would light up the dark skies
Illuminating all that was around me
I could see, and I saw what I thought was love
But at sunrise, the daybreak
That illumination seemed to fade away
Those same eyes that lit up my night
Seemed to darken my days
Those eyes blocked out the sun rays
And then I had no sight,
Again, in the midst of a beautiful sunny day
Birds chirping and the winds blowing,
whistling about singing praises
Flowers blooming, trees growing, minds elevated
All the while I could not see because of the dark
That was over me
That brought light to my nights
And darkness to my days
But I noticed when those eyes went away
I was able to see the sun on every new day
I hear the birds chant praises to Him
I feel the wind traveling from west to east
Seemingly aimlessly to the untrained mind
But all of it is a beautiful symphony
And realizing once I rid myself of those wandering eyes
Is when I began to walk into who I am meant to be
which is a child who is divine
And be a productive part of that symphony
That task, or privilege, that pleasure that is all mine

Part IV

Light

Days

Life has many phases
And there are many pages
 In that illustrious book
Sometimes some of the lines get mistook
Or mistaken
They cry enough tears to fill a brook
Yet they want to awaken
To days of enlightenment
But seem stuck
In a spiritual indictment
Of their own soul
Not knowing the role
They play in this novel
And their hearts grow cold
With no luck
Hoping for something exciting
But it is just them growing old
And it is frightening
Anticipating how the book will unfold
And how they'll be viewed by the Almighty
It is very daunting to the mind
And haunting to the brain
That all of what they sacrificed
Will never amount to gain
But they gave all their souls
Growing old as they continue to age
And in that book of life
They're afraid to turn the page
And live with anxiety, fear and rage
Of what will happen at their end of days

Fluid

Everything seems fluid
Waves transverse the many shores
With no obvious destination
Traveling round the land and merely waiting
With strain and tension
To be relieved of pain
Of burning during the transformation
Of boiling water and condensation
Reforming the vapor into rain
Only to start the cycle again
Reforming the vapor into rain

He Speaks

Who told you weren't good enough? You
Who told you that you were too old? You
I've been trying to speak to you
You can't hear because you are too into you
I have plenty of work in store for you to do
And plenty of blessings are awaiting you, too
But you're too busy being captivated by you
I created you better than all the things that you do
I told you that you were a god in Psalm 82
Don't act dumb, I watched you get it as your second tattoo
Now you wanna act like everything I said isn't true?
And have an issue with believing that I really love you?
You are my child, I would do almost anything for you
I sent My only begotten Son to die
You seriously don't believe I sat there and didn't cry?
He died for you and for you, I split the veil open wide
But let us take a step back and work with a fresh start
You won't feel Me completely until you trust Me with all
your heart

History

I won't be defined by my pain and misery
But I won't look at you and say it's all history
That it had no effect on shaping Henry
And the effects of what all that pain has meant to me
What I'm saying, quite simply
Is it's a difficult process fraught with many complexities
Getting myself back to a sane place, mentally
And not allowing medication to be the only remedy
But allowing my God to be a friend to me
Instead of being mad at Him like He's the enemy
Instead of running from Him and rushing nowhere on empty
Where can I go in this world that He can't get to me?
He's protected me when these girls tried tempting me
The tempestuous perils of a man named Henry

If He Loves Me

If He loves me, why does my soul seem to perish?
I cherish every moment with Him
Although to outsiders it isn't apparent
From drinking to womanizing and using vulgarities
It makes me fear the future ahead of me
To be specific, I'm talking eternity
I want to meditate in His Temple and hide in His Tabernacle
And behold His beauty every day after
Offer sacrifices in His tent with great shouts of praise
And hope when I see Him, He'll be pleased with all of my
days
I don't think He'll be pleased with all of my ways
And how I can't seem to make these demons go away
But I love Him, I really do love Him
Sometimes my life does not reflect it
But He promised me that a work He starts, He will perfect it

Life

I once said that L.I.F.E. is
Liars, Infidels, Fakes and Enemies
That's before I allowed myself
To experience my friend's love of me

So what is this L.I.F.E.?
Love Is Faith in Elohim
Not money, not cars
Not fulfilling earthly dreams

Not houses or jobs
Those are all man-made
It is all futile
Because we all end up in the grave

People spend a lifetime compiling wealth
Spending all their time until none is left
Then lie on their death bed feeling unfulfilled
And all their money is spent by someone else

People plan for retirement
Not knowing if today is their last
They sacrifice life to gain materials
But to be first, you must be last

God's hand remains unseen
Yet effects all of human history
He intervenes on behalf of man
His Word reveals some of His Mysteries

That which can be seen is first in the brain
But the last is what's invisible
So to have life, the first must be last
And the last shall be first, lest one is miserable

Man Under a Tree

There was an old man sitting under a tree
On a park bench
He peeled his apple and admired the leaves
Every day he told me something I didn't want to believe
That I was chasing prosperity, but it wasn't reality
I laughed at him, not understanding His wisdom and truth
I was a vibrant and virile youth
To me, it sounded like the words of a fool
Then one day the words hit me
When I was older of course
But when I went to find him and see
I found He was no longer under the tree
I thought that He was no longer to be
But realized He left the ninety-nine just to come and find me

Naked

Life is no more than a mist
You're here today, then suddenly no longer exist
In the physical
So why spend your time chasing these materials?
Everything you need, I provide
You don't need leaves, who told you that you were naked?
When will you get to the point that you stop faking?
You can't fool Me, for I know it all
I don't believe I told you to walk before you crawl
Why do you need someone to be in love with you?
When God Almighty is already in love with you
So tell Me why you feel the need to be approved?
And tell Me how you're always concerned with Two?
You disobey the things I tell you to do
Everything I tell you is for your benefit
I gave My Word, My Son, My people, My church, but you're
still not getting it
You are loved and no longer in the nude
Don't you know, in My heart, that you are my muse?
You don't seem to get most of My cues
Don't you know, on My team, there's no way you can lose?
Don't you know My intent is never to abuse?
I gave you clothes when you realized you were nude
Now, you're still doubting Me, really, dude?
You don't seem to understand I only want the best for you?
Like I said before, I don't even need the best of you
I already have your love, I just want the rest of you

Ode to a Star

The first time I laid eyes on you
When I saw you in that congested room
I knew what love was, that very second
I knew my life would never be the same
I knew you would call me by name
The first time I looked into your eyes, I knew
I would always be a different me
And that I would, if needed, die for you
When you lay your head on my chest
Drawing comfort and rest
You hear my heartbeat in your ear
At night, I'm delighted when you're near
We've grown so very close
Anytime you aren't here
About you, I shamelessly boast
Of how you bring a smile to my face
How you make me laugh
And how, sometimes, you make me mad
When I'm with you, there's nothing to compare
I've never told you about the void
I feel when you aren't there
I love you so much and I'm proud that you are mine
But every time I see you
I can't forget the first time

Rain

To me, water from the rain is life
With no rain, there is no food
With no rain, there are no vegetables and fruits
No flowers and trees, no grass and leaves
And not just for you
Even the animal's flesh you choose to consume
It's not the rain of Noah's day
Where everyone is erased, going away
Not the rain that drowns you
It's water of life that surrounds you
And all the joy that abounds in you
To me, water and rain are life

Rose Petals

The rain falls, the sun shines, the wind blows
And inevitably, the beautiful flower grows
With much care and love until it is nurtured into a bud
Then it blooms and is used as an expression of love
But there are thorns nearby to protect the prize
Once it is plucked from the vine, it eventually dies
The petals fall one by one to the ground
With its many stigmas searching around
To bring back the beauty that once was
Now nowhere to be found
Scattered about, tossed in the wind
Trampled under feet, never to be one again
With desire to save one for true expression of *amore*
But what was one, is now the possession of many
Except for one petal, that will not be given to any

Savior

The most beautiful thing in the world is You, Jesus
I would completely be nothing without you, Jesus
You were tortured and beaten, wearing thorns on Your head
For me, and I'm not worth You being dead
And rising
But when that sun rose on the horizon,
You woke up to give people like me life and
I'm forever grateful for Your fatal sacrifice and
I'll try not to be hateful, You paid too big a price and
Getting nailed to a cross while Your followers were crying
Or running away, not believing the third day You would rise
again
You're my brother, more than my friend
I am nothing without You, my precious LORD
I'm sorry when it seems like I'm not all onboard
I know I sin again and again, acting like I repent
I'm afraid of You finally cutting the cord
Oh LORD, I am trying, but my soul is hideous
Though to You is it's a gift that needs to be given and
I don't really understand all of Your ways
But I know I want to be with You for all of my days
I know You give me vision when my mind's in a haze
I know You keep my mind right when I'm in a craze
Your works in my life never cease to amaze
But why me? You know how wretched I am?
And You tell me You love me, You are the Great I AM

Showers

Today, I went outside to enjoy the rain
And I began to pray because
This day, my heart was colored gray
And tears drenched my sullen face
Then God came with His solemn grace
He didn't come to wipe my tears
This day, He cried His own rain
And told me not to fear
He hears my cries and pain
So He decided to cry beautiful tears of rain
The same as me
To show me comfort in my misery
To let me know I'm not alone, He cried along with me

Songs of Moshe I

Though my soul belongs to Him
Tears saturate my garments
They anoint my pages
Keep my face moist
For He loves me
Yet I feel unlovable
He forgives me
Yet I feel unworthy
He comforts me
Yet I feel alone
He listens to me
Yet I feel as if I will never have a friend
He heals me
Yet my heart still hurts
He is my Shepherd
So I shall not want
He has fulfilled my needs
But I am too hurt to see
He has been my friend
But I was too sad to notice
He healed my hurts
But I wouldn't let go of the pain
He answered my prayers
But I forgot what I prayed
Blessed is our Lord
For He never leaves us

Songs of Moshe II

I awake early in the morning
And I cry to Thee, oh Lord
Are you listening to me?
For my heart hurts every day
My eyes are filled with tears
My body aches from depression and fear
You are my provider
You are my comforter
Please don't hide Your face from me
I cannot survive without You
Please hear my prayers
Make my heart pure if it is wicked
Heal my body and my heart
Give me hope
Hear me because of the Blood of Your Son
Jesus is my Savior
Love me, O Lord, comfort me
I am weak and weary
Because of my sins, I am broken
I lost my love, I feel lowly
Make me whole, O Lord
Please do not ever leave my heart

The Truth Hurts

Some say you're a genius
You're just a regular person
Yes, you're good looking
But you aren't the only one in the world
Many more are better looking
You're kind, but you aren't the kindest
People give money, but more so, many give their lives
You aren't the most faithful, God took that crown already
You aren't the most athletic or you would've had a
professional career
You aren't the most poetic or you would be a bestseller
And your career path would be clear
You aren't a genius
You're a regular person with supernatural powers
You're a prophet from God Almighty Himself
But that role is not self-aggrandizing
It is humbling
And as humble as you believe you are, the fact is, you are
smug
You think because you own a home and three cars you aren't
a thug?
You think God saving you repeatedly from death is not
enough?
You think you aren't going to suffer from dipping all that
snuff?
Yes, you are a prophet, but your ego goes before you
You call yourself a lowly servant
But are you serving God or man?
For recognition from below or when you reach Heaven
Are you down for the struggle, down for the cause?
Or will you run whenever something gives pause?
You see, God isn't big on giving clauses

You're either in or you don't walk through doors
So, who are you, a saint or perpetual sinner?
Are you grounded in the Word or are you a beginner?
You only think about being a winner
But in which game do you participate?
You don't think God sees when you fornicate?
You think God is gonna bless you when you masturbate?
The crazy love He gives means He will
But you cannot continue to live outside of His will
And expect your purpose to be fulfilled
People say you're a genius, but you're just another person
That may not be what you want to hear, but the truth hurts

Why Me?

So often, I stare in the mirror
But I loathe the sight I see
So many say I'm beautiful
But they can't see inside of me
God sees my heart and still, He loves
Why me?

God asks for my obedience
But I always seem to go astray
And start dancing with the devil
But God always brings me back His way
He thinks about me every day
Why me?

When my heart is broken
He lends His tender touch
He turns my tears of tragedy
Into love that means so much
He never tells me He's had enough
Why me?

When it's time to rise for church
I lie in bed and hide
I'm scared that He will leave
So there's a woman by my side
He promises in my heart He will always reside
Why me?

After nights of drunken debauchery
He makes sure I get home safely
I do it so repeatedly
I feel for sure, He must hate me
But He never forsakes me
Why me?

Why me, why does He care?
I don't do anything but disappoint Him
I know I hurt His Heart
But I've been blessed and anointed
Even though I sin, I am His appointed
Why me?

It makes me hate myself worse
Because His love never wavers
It seems I never do what's right
Be He sent His Son as Savior
So that I, too, can be greater
Why me?

Your Beauty

How beautiful the clouds, how majestic are the skies?
Am I really that beautiful in Your eyes?
How wet is the water?
And how is my big Brother, Jesus?
When He sees me fuck up, does He have tears in His eyes

How beautiful the day, I gave my soul away
To You, God, and I reminisce on that day
I fell in love in with You
What happened that turned me into a fool?
I became an idiot that went astray

How beautiful the rain, the thoughts in my brain
How silly of me to hurt You when I'm going insane
But Your love remains
It seems my hurt can't be contained
I still enjoy all Your beauty in my pain

Your beauty in the clouds and majesty in the skies
Am I truly that beautiful in Your eyes?

CPSIA information can be obtained
at www.ICGtesting.com
Printed in the USA
LVHW090900230122
709159LV00006B/79

9 780578 996318